TRAINING TIPS
for
WESTERN RIDERS

TRAINING TIPS
for
WESTERN RIDERS

Volume 2

By **L. N. Sikes**

with **Bob Gray**

*A guide to the
knowledge and safe
use of western horses*

Photography by **Bob Gray**

Cordovan Corporation 1963
Cypress, Texas

The Cordovan Corporation
Cypress, Texas

Training Tips for Western Riders
Volume 2

COPYRIGHT (c) 1963
by
The Cordovan Corporation

FIRST EDITION

Library of Congress Catalogue Card No. 61-6567

Printed in the United States of America

Foreword

IT WOULD be difficult if not impossible for anyone to read a book like this and then go right out and, with no other experience, completely train a young horse. Experience is the best teacher in this field, as in most others. Words on paper can never be a complete substitute for experience.

Nor do the authors suppose for one minute that everyone who loves horses *wants* to train them. Some people are not constitutionally put together right to even try it. This is why the current national boom in horse use has produced many outstanding stock horse trainers. These men are professionals and have spent a lifetime studying horses and learning how to teach them. Veteran horsemen know that money spent on professional training is money well spent.

And yet there are few people who own horses who don't have the strong urge to do *some* training, at one time or another. If you are so inclined you must first understand the way horses think and behave at different ages, under different conditions. Equally important, you must understand *yourself* and what you need to learn before you can communicate with a horse.

Horses are quite different from our other domestic animals. They are more complicated creatures than dogs, more unpredictable than cats, far more intelligent than some people believe, yet less intelligent than many horse lovers believe. They react in a positive way to everything that humans do around them. We can train a horse and we can also, quickly, *untrain* one. Most spoiled horses are spoiled by man. Most mean horses get that way through mishandling by man. Horses, in short, are what we make of them.

Nor will you find horses like great anonymous herds of cattle. They are nearly all as different, one from another, as are humans. There are dumb horses and smart horses, lazy ones and energetic ones, temperamental horses and those with placid dispositions.

They aren't all the same—and they don't all *train* the same. This is why a human horse trainer must be a blend of patience, flexibility, curiosity, determination and understanding. We offer you this book in the hope that you will find these qualities in yourself as you work with one horse or many—and that some of these tips and suggestions may help you feel the tremendous personal satisfaction everyone experiences who has ever taught a horse to do something and do it well.

Bob Gray
Cypress, Texas
November, 1963

CONTENTS

1

Gentling The Colt

MOST people nowadays raise horses to show. They go see about their cattle in a Jeep. So they want their horses pretty gentle and a lot of people don't really know what to expect from a colt. Some think it's cute and funny for a colt to chew on them. If I'm going to feed one, I want him to eat that feed instead of chewing on me.

Colts can be taught something from the time they're a week old. But before he's a day old he won't know his mama from anything else. He'll want to go to anything that moves. If a colt is laying down and the mare walks away—and you happen to be standing near—the colt may jump up and come to you. A baby calf will do the same thing. He may even follow the horse you're riding.

A mare's personality can have something to do with how spooky a colt is. One thing you can do is feed this mare from a bucket and if she's pretty spooky don't feed her from anything *but* a bucket. Stay there with her until she eats all you give her. Then she'll always come to you. When her colt arrives, it won't take long for it to dawn on that colt what you're doing. He will start trying to eat some too. Then you can start putting your hands on him. Don't slap him or anything. Just scratch his tail up on the croup or at the base of the tail. Then you may get him gentle enough to rub up under his ears or on his throat. Most of them don't like to be patted between the eyes.

You may find some colts eating grain with their mothers when they're a week old. But some mares won't let their colts eat with them at all. I have an old mare like that. She has always been kind of a

A foal can be gentled early with feed and personal care. Most foals will start nibbling grain with their mothers at the age of a week or two, then can be haltered and taught to lead soon after.

greedy old thing and it didn't take her colts long to learn to stay out of her way. And if we didn't wean her colts by the time they were five months old, *she* weaned them. You can feed that kind of mare in a long feed trough so the colt can get a little something too.

We have quite a few colts around here so we don't mess with them quite as much as the average person who may have just one or two. But most colts raised in a pen or small pasture like to make friends. To gentle our own colts we will just walk around them a lot every day and feed them a mouthful of feed every time we get a chance. We won't scare a colt; just stand there and if he comes up, scratch him a little.

A child can gentle the average colt as quick as anybody. A colt is curious anyway and he'll walk up to a child if the child stays around long enough. The colt will get so curious he'll just have to come see what the child is doing. I've seen colts walk away from their mothers lots of times to see what I was doing. They're not all alike, of course. Some are born with a wilder nature than others and the colt that is raised out on the open range won't be so apt to be gentle as the one that is around people every day.

The more you're around a mare and colt the easier they get to handle. Even to loading them in a trailer. If the mare will load and you keep the colt where he can *see* his mother go in that trailer, so will the colt, if there's room. But if you put her in a covered trailer where she'll be hidden, then he may circle the trailer and not find her.

You want to slip a soft little halter on the colt when he's a week or so old. And the first time you catch a colt, it's better to be in a pretty close place. At first, he'll just run around you. Finally, he'll stop. Most colts you can catch right out in the pasture if the mare doesn't object. If he jumps away, don't follow him. Just wait until he starts nursing again.

Once you get the halter on a colt, you can lead him along behind his mother to get him used to leading. Do this every day for a little while and before long, he'll be used to you leading him. I wouldn't leave the halter on him all the time, though. He can actually stick his foot through that halter and he may get it caught there. A colt can just about scratch the top of his head with his hind foot, like a dog. I knew a roping horse once that a man left all the time with a neck rope on him. He was an active horse and he'd scratch his neck or ear with a hind foot. He got his foot through the neck rope one time and the rope wouldn't break. The horse stayed that way all night and it paralyzed the side of his head.

Another thing: A colt is always rubbing around on things and he sure may get that halter hung on something. Also, if you leave it on him all the time, it can make a ridge across his nose. You know what a trainer says—if a horse doesn't have a good nose or a good mouth, you don't have much else to handle him with.

Naturally, if he wears that halter all his life his nose will get tough and won't be sensitive when you start to break him to ride. I think I'd just put the halter on while I lead him. In two or three days of practice leading he'll get to where you can catch him and put the halter on pretty easy. The first three or four times may be a little trouble.

With enough handling, you can gentle a colt very early. We showed one in a halter show last year that was three months old. We took him away from his mama for about four hours to go to a show 10 miles away. It didn't bother the old mare very much, either.

Gentling The Colt

To show you what they'll do, my daughter Jan got to fooling with this colt and got it gentle. But the old mare was kind of hard to catch. So we decided one day to bring the mare and colt to the barn to put them in a stall. We couldn't catch the mare but the colt came right to Jan. She put the halter on it and began to lead the colt to the barn. Here came the old mare, following her colt. That won't happen often but it did that time.

Brushing and grooming is also good for a colt. By the time they're four or five months old they'll start shedding anyway and if you don't rub them they'll start rubbing on things themselves. The first place a colt will start shedding is around the eyes. Usually this is where you can first tell what color a colt will be. If a colt is born in the spring you can blanket him in the fall and bring out his natural color. He'll start getting slick and shiny then—if you continue to give him enough groceries and good exercise.

2

The Yearling

THE FIRST THING I notice about a yearling is his awkward-ness. Not always the way he *handles* himself but the way he *looks*. If he's a yearling that has raised himself out on pasture he may be a more awkward-*looking* pony, but lots of times he won't be that way in his actions.

A filly or horse colt (stud colt) of this age—from 12 to 24 months old—may look like a young teen-age boy. A boy may stumble and be all feet sometimes. His muscles aren't yet developed—in fact, he's not really developed anywhere. The filly will often be more developed as a yearling than a horse colt will. In fact, she may be as much developed as a yearling as a horse colt will at two years of age.

Some Aren't Awkward

Now I don't mean to say that *all* colts at this age are awkward. Let me give you an example: A man called me to his place once to see a bunch of about 12 fillies and colts. He told me which ones he liked best, the best-bred ones and all. He showed me one filly that was a good-looking filly but she looked awkward to me. He kept asking me what I thought of her.

"I like her all right," I told him, "but I don't think she can stand up." He said, "What do you mean, she can't stand up?"

So we ran her out in the hall of his barn and I sent a boy down to the far end with instructions to spook the filly when I ran her toward him. He did, and when the filly turned around, she fell down. He ran her back to me and when I spooked her, down she went again.

7

This man had a little ugly colt in this bunch, probably with no breeding at all and I asked him, "You want to see one you can't *throw* down?"

"You mean that thing?" he asked.

"Yes sir."

Well, you could spook that colt every way and make him jump in any direction and he'd just stop and spin around. He was as sure-footed as anything you could want. If the filly had been that agile no telling what she'd have been worth. But we had the action in the ugly colt and the looks in the filly. We did all 12 of the man's colts that way and it seemed like all the ones he liked would stumble and get their legs crossed.

"Well," he finally said, "from now on I won't go by the looks every time."

Disposition

You can also tell lots of times what kind of disposition a yearling will have when he's grown. But don't be fooled—a dog-gentle colt may not always turn out to be the best horse. You may find a yearling that will fight like a tiger the first time you tie him up. He resists every thing you try to do to him. In a way, I like that—if the colt has been out on pasture he has every reason to try and protect himself. But if he has always been around people and been handled enough to be halter broke and he *still* fights you, then he may be a high-tempered horse and hard to manage all his life.

If a yearling is a spooky kind of colt—wide-eyed and noticing everything—he'll probably be that way when he's grown. If you can

Most ranches will separate their horse colts and fillies by the time they are yearlings and it is in this important second year of life that horses are in a kind of animal adolescence—learning about other horses and the world around them.

jab him with your thumb and it takes him a little while to realize that somebody punched him, he's apt to be that way all his life too. I like for a colt to be alert. He has to be if he's going to amount to anything in contests.

I was talking to a man once about buying one of his colts and we were squatting on the ground near some yearlings in a pen. While we talked I began to take some pebbles and thump them over toward the colts. I noticed this bay colt watching every pebble. This man thought I was just playing with the rocks. But every time I thumped a rock this bay colt was the only one to see it. When it hit the ground he'd cut his eyes around and stick his ears toward that noise.

Finally, the man asked me which colt I wanted to buy.

"That poor colt over there," I told him.

He laughed and kidded me then.

"If I'd known you didn't know any more about horses than that I'd have *given* him to you."

"Well, you *can* give him to me," I told him.

Anyway, I took the colt home and my oldest boy Sonny broke him and started him as a cutting horse. Later, Clem Boettcher of East Bernard, Texas, bought him and named him Sonny Sikes after the boy. He's been a good cutting horse ever since and has sold a couple of times for high prices—once for about $5,000. The horse is now 18 years old.

9

The Yearling

Stall Versus Open Range

In most places you don't see many horses that haven't been halter-broke by the time they're yearlings. Especially if they're registered horses that will be shown. But some of the best horses I ever saw weren't halter-broke until they were two. In some of the range areas —places like West Texas—they run out and make their own living. Nature helps to take care of those horses. They learn a lot about life and how to protect themselves. The horse raised out there in the woods or among the rocks has to watch out for rattlesnakes and coyotes, for instance. Lots of these stall-raised colts wouldn't know a rattlesnake from a buggy-whip. They might just walk up and smell one. The range colt will also find he can't run a mile to water. If you turn a stall-raised pony out he's liable to run so long he'll make himself sick and maybe take cold.

I've broken and ridden both kinds of horse and the range pony catches on quicker if he's a little bit wild at first. The stall pony is expecting to be petted while the range horse will try to do what you want him to after he finds out you're in charge. He's got a little more "want-to" in him because he's been on the go all his life.

So the more you can keep a yearling out on range or pasture, the better horse it will make. Of course, the better the grazing the better job of growing the young horse can do. In places like West Texas and Kansas, where there is much lime in the soil, a colt can get quite a bit of his growth as a yearling. And this is another place where Nature can raise horses better than humans can.

You can feed young horses so well in stalls—with all the minerals they have now—that a colt can be *too* big by the time he's a two year old. He may have too much weight for what his feet can comfortably carry at that age. Out on pasture he may get grass-fat but

not *that* fat. Out in the open he can walk off his excess fat and develop more muscle. (See chapter seven.)

Also, on pasture he's less apt to develop a thick neck if it's a stud
colt. The young stud raised in a stall can develop a neck like a bull's
—unless you put his feed trough on the ground. The stud colt out
on pasture has to keep his neck down while he's eating and his neck
won't get as big and his withers have a chance to develop.

In a stall, most horses will eat out of troughs at waist-level or look
out of windows at the same height. This is why you see so many flat-
withered, thick-necked horses in stalls. That horse has it too easy.

It's hard, of course, to keep a yearling in show shape and still keep
him on pasture. Naturally, you don't want him out in the hot sun
all day if you're trying to keep his coat looking good. But you can
keep him up in the hot part of the day and then turn him out to
pasture in the evening and at night. And if you must have him in
the stall part of the time, put his feed box on the floor. That'll keep
some of the 'big' off his neck.

Speed of Development

The sex organs begin developing in horses when they're yearlings.
Most fillies will start coming 'in season' when they're six or eight
months old and I have a few cases where a stud colt of 12 or 13
months would breed a mare and get a colt. I also once owned a
mare that had a colt when she was two. But this tends to stunt the
growth of a mare and is pretty dangerous.

Speed of development depends on how you keep your horses. If
you run a bunch of yearling stud colts together they won't develop
as fast. But you keep a stud colt in a stall by himself he'll start to
get rowdy and maybe even mean—and he'll start to act like a stud.
Nearly everyone separates their stud colts and fillies into separate
pastures when they're yearlings, and lots of people separate them
when they're weaned—at about six or seven months.

As yearlings, the fillies will learn a little faster than the stud colts.
Usually they're not quite as headstrong too. If a filly decides not to
do something, you can usually make her do it. Correct her and she
may get a little bit sour, back her ears and show signs of being aggravated. The horse colt probably won't act that way.

He'll just be a little tougher and take more punishment than the
filly. In other words, you can make her do something she doesn't

*The more young horses can be kept on good open range
or pasture the better it may be for their future health
and stamina. In the rocky hill country near New Braun-
fels, Texas, McDannald Ranch horses (left) develop
stout feet and self-reliance.*

want to do and she'll show it. It won't make the stud colt as mad
to do something he doesn't want to do—but it won't be as easy to
make him do it.

Still, the filly will catch on quicker than the horse. She'll probably
remember it better too.

A Pleasure to Watch

I like to stand and watch these yearlings in a pasture. They'll run
and play kind of like little kids. They try to outdo each other in
running, especially—for no reason at all and usually at the same
place every day they'll all break into a run.

If you watch every day, you'll notice there will be one who wins
nearly every time. Then there will be one clown in the bunch that
doesn't care *when* he gets there. He figures there'll be some feed left
anyway.

This is a 'nosey' age too. If a yearling sees something in the pasture
he hasn't seen before—whether it's a paper sack or a person—he has
to go see about that. That's why it is risky to leave a car and trailer
around yearlings in a pasture. One of them will be sure and try to
walk *between* the car and the trailer, just to see if he can. If he does
try, another may nip him as he goes through and force him to jump
across the hitch. Whatever it is, you can be sure a yearling will nose
around it.

Hard To Judge

This is an especially hard age for people to judge a horse, if they
haven't seen a lot of colts grow up. After you have seen some grow,
you will get a pretty good idea of what others will do. And if you're
starting to breed horses, there's no use kidding yourself. Some people
will take an old sorry mare and breed her to a good horse and expect
the colts to look just like that stud. And when they're yearlings those
folks will start looking for—and sometimes finding—all kinds of good
things about poor colts. But a colt won't get here without a mama.
And she's going to mark him too.

3

The Two-Year-Old

THE two-year-old is in one of the most attractive stages that a horse goes through. As a yearling, he was in sort of an awkward stage. He's apt to look awkward again as he goes from a three to a four-year-old. But at two he will 'bloom.' He'll be old enough to ride —although not old enough to do a lot of hard work—and you can start to find out what the horse is good for.

Most people outside of the horse business can't tell a two from a three-year-old. Actually, if you look in his mouth just before he's two you will find he has about the same kind of teeth that he will have at five. He has a full set of teeth in front—except they are baby teeth. When he is three, a year later, he will have some of his baby teeth left but there will be two permanent teeth in front on the top and bottom. He will have all his permanent teeth at five.

Experienced horsemen can tell a two-year-old just to look at him. His features make him look more like a colt than a grown horse. And I don't think there's much of anything prettier than a two-year-old filly.

I've seen some two-year-olds that could stand about as much work as a four-year-old. But most of them should not get that much. In fact, if you have a horse this age that really *wants* to do something in a contest, you have to be careful to keep from letting him overdo it. A colt that tries real hard can hurt himself. He doesn't know how much he can stand.

At two, a young horse is out of the awkward stage but not yet fully-grown. He is part colt and part horse. He is not old enough yet for a lot of work but he is ready to be ridden and to start his performance training.

What a Two-Year-Old Can Do

I have seen two-year-olds stop and jerk cattle, if they had any size to them, just like a grown roping horse. You may rope three or four calves on a colt like that and he will enjoy it. But if you rope two more calves on him he may not like it anymore. He may not want to run them.

Don't ever figure that horses aren't smart. A two-year-old can find a lot of ways to get out of doing things, pretty quick.

I remember a two-year-old stud colt I was pretty proud of here a few years ago. I decided finally that he was ready to go to his first cutting. He had been doing real good at home. So I loaded him up and took him down to Tyler. It was his first trip away from home. When it came my time to work I thought the colt was getting a good job done but directly he just stopped and threw his head up. Then he looked back over the back fence and squealed. Everybody laughed, of course. I said, "Now you can laugh—but I bet there's a cow out there, *somewhere.*"

Also, I've seen young cutting horses go straight across that pen, running an old cow just right, looking square into her eyes. Then the cow will stop and turn back—and the horse will keep right on going. What probably causes this is that a colt has been worked too hard and now he doesn't like it too good. He thinks to himself, "Well, I just don't have to head her this time." And he'll try you that way, figuring he'll get by with something.

The Two Year Old

So, to get the best out of a two-year-old, you have to know him as an individual. What kind of personality he has also will depend on whether the colt is a mare or stallion.

Behavior By Sexes

The stud colt, at two years, is about like a 15-year-old boy. That colt is beginning to look at mares and he'll be more bull-headed than a filly. He is capable of more work than a filly but he doesn't learn as quick as she does. One day he'll work like a champion, the next day he'll look like a chump.

In the old days when horses ran in big herds on range country, an old stallion would chase off all the two year old stud colts. The older stud didn't want those youngsters around. Those were *his* mares and he usually wouldn't even let a strange mare join the band.

Now you'll find pastures full of stud colts—and two is the age at which most are gelded. Farmers used to wait until a horse was three before gelding, "to make more horse." They thought that a horse with a big neck was what they wanted. The extra age may have made his shoulders better for work purposes—but the cowboys sure didn't want big-necked horses. They didn't care how much muscle he had in the hindquarters as long as he wasn't bull-headed. And usually you stop that neck growth if you geld at two.

The two-year-old Paint stallion (center) gets an education in living as he goes into a pen with three older geldings. They won't take any nonsense from him . . .

16

If I think a colt is a stud prospect I don't like to start breeding him and training him for something at the same time. If you start him in training, with no breeding, you can carry him right on and he won't act near as much like a stud. Even among the race horses they are sometimes four or five years old before they breed them.

If you decide to start breeding a stud colt, I wouldn't breed him to more than 10 or 12 mares his first year. That's plenty. I don't think you'd want to pasture-breed that many. It would be best, I think, not to turn him out with more than four or five mares. It doesn't hurt either to turn him out with mares that already are in foal. A young stallion can learn a lot from this. By the time he gets kicked around by those mares, he can be very well-mannered. But for that purpose, I'd rather put a two-year-old stud with a bunch of geldings. Naturally he will try to pick a fight with some of them—and if they are older than he is, they can make a believer out of him pretty quick. He's just another horse to them and he will wind up a lot easier to handle around other horses.

With these young stallions, the more freedom you give them, the less trouble they'll give you. If nothing else, try to put a colt in a pen big enough so he can work off a lot of that vim. We ride most of our studs and the ones we don't ride we turn into a pen and make them run and trot. I've got a pen with deep, heavy sand in it and

. . . and soon the Paint is just one of the crowd. If he doesn't bother the geldings they won't bother him and he becomes a lot easier to handle around other horses.

17

this will muscle a horse pretty good. With every step he's got to pick his feet up high enough to clear that sand. (See Chapter Five)

How Fillies Act

Now as far as the way a filly acts at two, you'll find she is apt to try to do things you want her to a little harder than a stud. She will catch on quicker, too. And where you may have to spend an hour or two getting a stud warmed up, with his mind on what you're fixing to do, a filly may be ready to go right from the barn into a working pen and do what she's supposed to.

The two-year-old filly will be having more regular heat periods in her second year. At that time, she may get ill-tempered, may wring her tail and back her ears. Sometime she may kick when a rider spurs her at this time. Some fillies will go right ahead and work, even during those heat periods.

People are breeding quite a few fillies now at the age of two. I don't care much about doing this, unless a mare is already pretty big. If she has most of her growth it won't hurt her. In fact, it can age her some and settle her down. But ordinarily I would rather wait until a mare is three before I breed her. It gives her a little more time to fully develop. Besides that, most mares that are bred at two have poor first colts anyway. The rest of her colts will usually outgrow that first one. One reason for this is that she probably won't give as much milk when her colt arrives as she will when she is older.

4

The Three-Year-Old

AT THREE, your colt will be getting to be a lot more like a horse. He may still have "colty" ways. It depends on what you do with him.

For instance, there's a riding club near where I live and one man in it has a black grade horse. He does whatever comes into his mind when he gets on that horse. If he wants to run barrels on him, he runs barrels. If he wants to run the flag race, he does it. If he wants to rope calves, he ropes. Anything he decides to do on that horse, he tries—and he tries to make the horse do it right.

That colt is making a pretty good horse at most everything. He's not outstanding at any one event but he can go to those 'playdays' and do a little of anything that the rest can do.

Sex Makes a Difference

Naturally, your three-year-old mare won't react to this the same as a stallion. If you try a whole lot of things on a mare this age she may sour up on you once in awhile.

In the spring—from March on through the end of the breeding season—the young stallion wants everybody and everything to *know* he's a stallion. He's a lot like a rooster. And he'll be a little more aggravated at the things you want him to do. He will be looking off across some pasture at a mare much of the time and he may not like it if you turn him the other way. Some studs will cut up at this age and some won't. Full brothers will usually be of about the same temperament.

Compared to humans, a three-year-old will be roughly like a

young man or woman. They aren't in their prime yet but they are going into adulthood. As far as breeding is concerned, both mare and stallion are ready for production. The stallion will probably be as fertile at three as he will ever be.

When you start breeding the stallion you can expect that he will get more rank and harder to handle—unless you turn him out with a band of broodmares. That will quiet him a lot. If you can't turn him out with mares, then you should make him behave and not squeal and cut up when he's around them—or *try* as best you can.

Behavior at this age will also depend on how you have handled them up to now. If you catch colts in the pasture from the time they are yearlings and they are good gentle ponies, there won't be too much difference as they get older. But after a stud is three, he may not tolerate a gelding in the pasture with him. And after that horse is past three, there's probably not enough room in that pen for him and *another* stallion.

What the stallion learns at three will probably stay with him longer than the things he learned as a two-year-old. There are some things, of course, they don't ever forget no matter at what age they learn it. One thing is breaking the horse to tie. This is something they sure ought to know by the time they are three.

Your colts should be taught as soon as they're weaned to stay tied without breaking loose. If you tie one to a post or a fence and he breaks loose four or five times, he'll get to thinking he can break loose anytime he wants to. Also, you'd want to tie him higher than the withers—at least six inches higher—so he won't be so apt to pull the head down. By that, I mean a horse with a head 'pulled down' has spooked back against a stout rope tied lower than his head and it has pulled a joint loose. This kind will seldom carry the head right any more. He'll get over it but it can leave a sunk place in the neck.

As for mares at three, the female may not always learn any faster than a stallion but she will remember better. You can also develop her fast, in conformation, at three. If you have just let her run out and have not done anything with her, she might not have developed much by this time. But if you feed her good and give her plenty of exercise she'll be an altogether different-shaped mare at the end of her third year.

Training

This is the year to give this colt a good start—and how you start him can be the making of the horse. It is time to impress on his mind what you want him to do and try your best to get him to *like* it. We will talk more in another chapter about how you may want to do this.

Where I see a lot of trouble—with three-year-olds especially but with other ages too—is that many horses have had it too easy, just like people. They don't have enough nerve and "stay." Maybe we just ought to call it Guts. They may work all right when you're

The three-year-old is like a young man or woman— not yet in his prime but rapidly becoming an adult.

making them work but when you quit cueing and clucking, they quit working.

Sometimes in cutting cattle, as long as the cattle keep a colt interested, he looks good. But with lots of three-year-olds, if the cattle don't keep them real busy, they'll look away and slack off.

Part of the reason for this may be that we've been breeding for conformation a long time. The horses are being "bred up." Here lately we've also been breeding for speed to go along with this conformation—and I think that could help a lot. It should add more "staying power" to our contest and ranch horses too. So I think this problem will work itself out. In the next few years I expect we'll have some of the best looking performance horses that we've ever had. There will probably be more good-looking geldings around than Texas ever saw. Reason I think this is because of all the big two and three-year-old stallion classes you see at the shows. A lot of those will wind up as geldings.

By the time a horse is three, if you've ridden him off and on since he was two, you will just about have made up your mind what you want him to do. More than likely you will be doing it on him. At the end of his third year he should be able to win or place in a cutting horse contest or a roping, reining or a western pleasure class.

The Three Year Old

In other words, he's big enough and stout enough to go through whatever schooling or contest you put him in.

A Time to Buy

This is also a good age at which to buy a horse. Somebody will have spent a lot of time, and maybe money, starting this horse and you *know* somebody has spent some money on hay and perhaps feed to develop him. (If they haven't he'll show it!)

You can also tell from the cuts and scars on him whether he has been nosey or not. Some horses are just born to be meddlesome. They'll walk up and step in something just to see if they can walk through it. At three you can be sure this colt will have run over all the loose things in the pasture—he will already have cut one of his feet or as many of them as he's ever going to!

I once had a friend in Cameron, Texas, who had a horse like that. They could hardly keep him sewed up and all together until he was old enough to ride. They finally named him Aches and Pains, and he carried that name all his life. Yet he wound up making a good horse and lived to an old age.

5

Daily Exercise

THE way most people raise horses now—afraid to turn them out for fear they'll get hurt (and sure enough, they will)—they don't get ridden too much. They're kept in stalls and backyards and little pens. Horses need more exercise than they can get in a stall. They need it to develop their bodies, all over. Exercise also will keep a horse from being agitated and nervous, from walking the stall all day.

But the biggest trouble most people have is that they'll exercise a horse one day and tomorrow they don't have time. They'll overwork him today and tomorrow they won't work him at all.

Even a horse that hasn't been broke to ride needs exercise if you're keeping him in a small pen or stall. And when you start it you need to keep it up every day. This is sure true for a horse you're going to show at halter. It takes more than plenty of feed to bring out the best in a horse; in three weeks of working a horse in a pen you can tell a lot of difference. That exercise can get their hair in shape and their bodies looking a lot better.

It doesn't take so long—say 20 or 30 minutes a day—if you have a little pen you can use to work the horses in. It can be anywhere from 50 up to 70 feet square. I like to work from five to eight horses at a time in such a pen, but you can work one horse like that just as well.

Moving his horses around him in a trot, the trainer can exercise a number of animals well in less than half an hour. Many horses soon come to enjoy this.

The best gait he can go is a trot. He's working all his muscles the same and it also will improve his stride. A little horse that takes short, choppy steps can be exercised this way and made to lengthen his stride. He should be made to trot as fast as he can without breaking into a lope.

Start out easy with him and don't try to trot a soft horse 30 minutes the first day. Trot him five minutes and then add two or three minutes to it each day until you get him up to 30 minutes. After four or five days of this a horse will know what you want him to do in that pen and when you turn him loose and step out into the middle, he'll start in a circle.

To keep him moving I use a long bullwhip with a piece of rope or heavy string on the end that will make a loud popping sound. You don't need to hit the horse with this of course. It's the noise that makes him move along. After you start him it's not any trouble keeping him going.

Horses worked like this pick up some amusing habits. If you work several together it won't be long before each one will pick a buddy he wants to follow. Lots of times I've had them get in pairs and there will be some that want to be in front and some that want to be behind. They don't step on each other's feet as much as you'd expect either. In that circle they're moving at an angle.

If you happen to have a water trough in the pen where you work them, they'll also start trying to sneak a drink, just like a bunch of kids. I usually let them get away with one or two drinks of water—but you can expect that some start wanting a drink every time they make that circle.

Then there will be one that's a bossy kind of horse. He'll be agitated about having to take that exercise anyway and since there's nothing he can do about it, he may try to nip or kick at another horse just to take his spite out on *somebody*.

They'll get to know just about when you're supposed to quit too and they'll start watching you. They'll test you every once in awhile. They'll slow down and you can see them thinking, 'Well, it's about time to stop.' So when they get real tired you can holler 'Whoa' and they'll *all* hear you. They'll get broke to that 'Whoa' just like they will anything else. And you can put a new horse in with others that have been working like this before and he'll pick it all up pretty quick.

If there is a water trough in the exercise pen, you can bet that horses, like kids, will start sneaking a drink every chance they get.

Daily Exercise

After you've done a horse like this for 15 days or so he can trot 30 minutes and it won't hurt him at all. He'll get to where he likes it, in fact, and looks forward to it. You take one in there you've trotted quite a bit and he may not be able to wait until you take his halter off. He gets to wanting to go, right now. It's a lot of fun for him— for about five minutes. Then it runs into work.

The first few times you work a horse this way do it until he breaks a light sweat. He will sweat too—almost as much as if you were riding him. Afterward, the main thing is not to let him cool off too quick. Put a blanket on him if it's winter. If in the summer, don't tie him out in the hot sun. When you're through exercising him, walk the horse awhile and then tie him in the shade. He'll cool off pretty quick.

I've got one horse I call Pokey (his real name is Poco Nifty) and I guess he enjoys this kind of thing about as much as he does anything. He's a calm horse and about the only thing that upsets him is an empty feed trough. I can put him in that pen by himself and as soon as I take the halter off he takes off around that pen. He hits a stride he could hold half a day. He starts off like he might have to do it that long too—then when he gets tired he'll go to cutting his eyes at me. Finally when I holler 'Whoa,' he tries not to go another step.

6

Breaking and Starting
The Young Horse

WE'RE now past the stage when, to break a horse, you just went out and threw a saddle on his back. That way, you found out who was toughest, horse or rider. I never was that tough myself. But I have gone to get horses to break—and rode them home. Some bucked me off, of course. And if you hear a man say he never was bucked off a horse, you can be sure it's because he never rode any.

In the days before we had all the trailers and equipment like we have now it was sure different. If a man had some broncs that needed breaking, and if he could catch and saddle those horses himself, he wouldn't need anybody to help him. Horse-breaking jobs I'd get then meant the owner usually couldn't even catch the broncs to start with.

Toughest horse I ever met was at Belton, Texas, about 20 miles from where I lived as a boy. I traded for this mare and she had a saddle on already. It took three of us to get that saddle off and my saddle on her. Then, about sundown, I started home. I met a bunch of bridges and things—and I think we went around some of them. It was the wildest ride I ever made. After seven or eight miles she began to weaken enough to let me keep her in the road. By the time I got home she was almost broke to ride.

But I found out early that a horse that's tough to break can make you a good horse. I went to break two mares for a man one time and he thought these mares were four-year-olds. We found out later the man was a little boy when those mares were four. They were actually about 14 years old. They fought like wildcats after we caught them but they broke all right and made good horses. That fellow went right to farming with one of them. Those mares had a lot of sense and knew more about how to take care of themselves than a young horse.

So if the young colt you decide to break has some spunk and resists what you want to do with him, don't be disappointed. Look at it from *his* standpoint. Why should he want that halter on him? Or the saddle, either? He doesn't have any idea what you're fixing to do with him. So you sure don't want to have a fight with a colt just because he tries to protect himself. You want him to respect you but still not be so afraid of you that he tries to run from fright, rather than because he has some spirit.

Gentling and Leading

First, get the colt in a close place where you can pet him and rub him. Let him rub his head around on you all he wants to. It won't be but a few days before he does this anyway. If, after you get a halter on him, he doesn't want to lead, just walk around him. Turn him with the lead rope as you go, turning him round and round. Get the circle a little bigger each time and it won't be but 15 or 20 minutes before he will follow you away from that spot.

When you lead the colt away from other horses and people, off by himself, he's apt to be a little easier to handle. There won't be many other things to look at and he may kind of take up with you. After you have handled him awhile, petted him, rubbed your hands over him and talked to him, he should get the idea that you are his only protection. It would be a good idea to spend an hour or two at a time with him. Fool with him an hour or so in the morning and the same again in the afternoon—just leading him, picking up his feet, brushing him. This can go on for two or three days if you want to take it slow and easy so as not to hurry the colt.

Saddling

Before putting the saddle on the colt, I'd lay a blanket on the colt. Put the blanket on his back from one side, then go around and take it off from the other. You want him used to your working with him from both sides. After awhile, tie the stirrups together on top of the saddle and *lay* the saddle on his back. If those stirrups flopped loose and you swung it up on him, that stirrup or girth might fly over and hit him on the leg or knee. Take the saddle off after a few minutes, then put it back on again. Do this several times. After that, tie the front girth but don't pull it real tight. Just barely pull it up. I like to attach the flank or rear girth too, but not too tight. It's best to get the colt used to both girths now—if you don't put the flank girth on until later, then it is something new and it will take longer for him to get used to it.

Once saddled, lead him around a little bit. If he does well, back him a few steps. Naturally, few horses at this stage will want to back up. Every backward step he takes that flank girth will touch him on the belly.

Some youngsters may want to break a colt by riding him bareback. It does gentle him to ride bareback—but I've seen about as many sore-backed horses from bareback riding as from saddles on them.

Riding bareback is good for a child since it teaches them balance. And if they don't ride a colt too long bareback it won't hurt him. But there's no advantage to *breaking* one bareback. The rider's weight is all in one spot whereas the saddle spreads weight over a wider area of his back.

Bits

Most horses will resist the bit a little and will probably chew on it for awhile before he gets used to it. One way to get him used to it is to put a slick bit on him in his stall. Don't put any reins to the bit—just the bit and headstall—and make sure there are no projections in there for him to hang the bit on.

Then when you're teaching him to get used to the saddle, you can put the bit on and tie the reins over the saddle horn, making sure they are the same length. Tie the end of each rein to the D-ring on the saddle, on each side, to make sure the horse will carry his head straight and down. Be sure you have a curb strap or chain on it so he can't pull the bit through his mouth. He will naturally work his head down to get some slack in the reins—and before long will carry the head down at the right level when he has the bit on him.

I know some experienced horsemen, though, who never did learn to put a bit in a horse's mouth without a fight. I've seen men walk up to a horse, from straight in front, holding that bridle out in front of them like they think it's a window and the horse is supposed to stick his head through. Not many horses will do it.

I'd rather stand on the horse's left side, hold the top of the bridle with my right hand, over his neck, and guide the bit into his mouth with my left hand. If he doesn't want to open his mouth just press on his gum with one of your left hand fingers and he will open his mouth. If he's especially stubborn, touch the inside roof of his mouth with a finger. He will open up and lots of horses get to where they

A bit is apt to gag a colt (left) at first and he wants to get it out of his mouth. Securing equal-length reins to the saddle (right) helps him get used to it. You can handle him with the halter lead rope without having to use the reins.

open when the bit touches the mouth. It sure won't help, though, if you walk up and jab that bit in as though you were trying to poke a stick in his mouth.

Driving the Colt

The next step I'd recommend is driving the colt ahead of you with long lines. The photos show how you can do this. Tie the stirrups together under his belly, not tight, and run ropes through the stirrups to his hackamore or bridle. Start off with someone leading the colt while you get behind. After he's been led back and forth, 50 yards or so, two or three times, you can drive him almost any place you want to go. But it is better to do this in a small pen. When you practice stopping him, always call out "Whoa" before you put pressure on the lines.

After the person leading turns his head loose, keep him headed into a fence so he won't try to run off with you. When you turn him around, try to make him take a step or two back before you turn him. This will teach him to turn on his hind feet. If he does get scared and wants to run, guide him into a fence and stop him.

I would drive him with both a bit and a hackamore. But the bit isn't used to guide him. I just put an old work bit in his mouth so he can start getting used to a bit and bridle. The hackamore goes over that. In a few days you can run the long lines to the bit and use that to drive him.

If you will drive this colt every day for a week, about an hour a day, it will teach him so much that you can get on him and ride him. More than likely he won't buck at all. This is good. I figure the more they buck, the more they learn how.

With lines slack at first the colt gets used to ropes touching the body and on hind legs (above) while being led. While turning (left) keep light tension in both lines so body will stay straight.

Colt pictured on page 29 is being ridden here for first time. Most well-mannered colts today will not buck or pitch when first ridden if handled slowly and easily.

First Time On

Most colts that have been well-gentled won't get scared when you first get on. You can sit there and he will watch you and it doesn't bother him a whole lot to have you on his back—until he moves. When he moves and finds you still up there, it may excite him. So I'll usually tie a colt to a wall or fence, then get on and get off a few times. Then we will let someone hold the colt while I get on and off. Finally, we'll let another man lead the colt while there's a rider on his back. The man leading can talk to the colt and keep him from being excited. The colt can be wearing both bridle and bit and a halter, with the lead rope connected to the halter.

When the man leading the colt turns him loose, he should pet the colt, stop and hand the lead rope up to the man in the saddle. The colt thinks the man on the ground is still going to lead him. When the leader walks away the colt will probably follow him, and may keep following him up and down the pen. I'd ride the colt like this for 15 or 20 minutes, not trying to make him rein or do anything, but just getting him used to the weight on his back and how to carry it.

The thing to do is not try to put him in the 3rd grade when he is still in kindergarten. You'll wind up with a better horse if you just coax him along with these first few things rather than set your head and decide you're going to *make* him do something special.

I have seen three and four-year-old horses that somebody rushed too much that never were any good. A man may have a real good idea of what *he* wants a colt to do but the horse may have no idea at *all*.

You can expect that no horse will do everything you want him to the first time. He would rather be turned loose to start with. Now I don't mean stand around and do nothing but pet a colt. I do mean go slow and try to remember that the colt will know nothing but what he learns from you.

Reining

First thing lots of people want to do on a horse is to see how good he can be made to rein. They've watched these cutting horse men spin their horses around in a circle and they think this colt ought to do that. Well, the first thing that colt has to learn is to *go*, and go straight. Then comes stopping and turning.

31

Breaking The Young Horse

If you spent some time driving your colt with the lines, he learned a lot about what the signals to turn right and turn left felt like. He should have learned to answer the reins. Once you are on his back, you need to teach him to carry your weight and maneuver under it. Most horsemen cue their horses to go forward with their knees. They squeeze and release for the 'go' signal.

As he travels, keep a light pressure in his mouth, or if you're using a hackamore, on his nose. The first thing some riders do wrong is to rein the colt out on his neck or in the middle of his ears. Remember to do your reining over the saddle horn. Some trainers will hold one rein in each hand as they start a colt to reining. The important thing is that pressure should first be applied by the rein on the side you want him to turn toward. He won't know at first what to make of that other rein across his neck.

If you hold the reins in one hand and swing them to the right, say, the left rein will get tight first and the horse feels pressure in his mouth to the left. So he turns his head to the left when you're really wanting him to turn right. Just remember to keep the rein a little tighter in the direction you want to go.

This "putting a rein" on a horse is something you don't do in 30 minutes. You can take a bronc horse and put him in a small pen and, with some work, he may look like an experienced reining horse. But take him out into a 100 acre pasture and he won't look so good. Those fences in a pen can help a lot.

Stopping

When first breaking the colt, you want him to know what *stop* means. You want him to hear your voice command, "Whoa," and feel the backward pressure of your body in the saddle before you pull on the reins. In time, he should get to where the shift of your weight and the voice command will stop him with very little rein pressure. When the colt gets tired he will listen for that command and should be much easier to stop.

If the horse won't try to stop, you can head him into a fence or a corner. Just before he gets there, pick up on him just enough so that he knows you want him to stop. The fence will finish the job. Not many horses will hit the fence. I have seen a few butt it like a goat. But not many times.

When you put rein pressure on him to stop, do it low and directly over the saddle horn. Pull toward your stomach and keep his head straight as he stops, but not continuously. Pull, then release.

It is a good thing to work this colt with a hackamore until he gets to pulling against it. As you stop him, he may root with his head and not respect the hackamore. That's when you should go into a snaffle bit or a hackamore bit with shanks on the bottom.

Early Habits

A young horse when first started, after the first few days of training, will try to do what you want him to. It's usually too much trouble for him to do otherwise. If he knows you just want him to walk down the road, he'll get to doing that.

The colt will do other things for you too. That first week he will be apt to cross bridges all right, perhaps even go down and cross ditches. The second week he'll do pretty much what you want too. He's so sore from carrying you the less he can do the better it suits him. About the third or fourth week he is over that soreness and is beginning to wise up. He gets smart and starts showing *you* what to do. That's when you may start having problems with him. It is almost as though he were telling you, "Aw, let's don't do it that way; let's do it like *I* want to!"

He may decide, for instance, that he doesn't want to turn one way or the other. Usually he will turn easier to the left. This is because most riders hold the reins in their left hand and naturally it is more convenient for them to rein to the left. If you want to encourage him to rein to the right, put your left hand out alongside his head as you rein to the right and shift your weight over into the right stirrup. A lot of effective reining is done by shifting your weight.

The colt may also develop the habit of starting to walk off as you prepare to mount. Make him stand still until you get on. In fact, get on and off enough times so he will understand that he is not to move until you cue him.

Leads

This word means whichever feet a horse is 'leading' with in a lope. If he is in a right hand circle, he should be leading with his right forefoot and his right hind foot should be coming up under him at the same time. In a left lead his left forefoot and right hind foot hit the ground at the same time. If he is on the proper lead he is loping easily; he lopes rough and awkwardly if he isn't.

Yet some horses, exercised in a pen, will lope on the wrong lead in a circle, even with no rider on them. Like people, some colts are just awkward. If I'm exercising colts in a pen and I see one on the wrong lead, I'll pop my whip and maybe step in front of him. He'll gather himself usually and get on the proper lead. Eventually most colts will pick up leads themselves when they find it is easier to lope that way.

When you start riding a colt, you need to pay attention to which lead he is on as you begin loping him. In a straight trot there is no lead since that is a 'square' gait. In a circle, the trotting horse will lead the same as he would in a lope.

If you are loping a colt and find him on the wrong lead, you need to either break his stride by pulling him back into a trot, or else stopping him. As you start him out again shift your weight in the direction you want to go and rein him that way. He should step off with the proper foot.

The best instruction at first is to ride the colt in a straight line, perhaps down a road. Then, in a pen at least 50 to 75 feet across,

In left lead the horse leads left forefoot while left hind foot comes forward. Rider has slightly more pressure in left stirrup. Good leads are essential to contest excellence and riding comfort.

lope him in a circle. Stop him occasionally, turn him to the outside of the circle and lope the other way. Work to keep him in the proper lead and correct him if he's not. I have seen some trainers, with bad-leading horses, do this: Angle your colt slightly to the right, say, of the direction you want to go. Then rein him sharply to the left and shift your weight to the left, to get him started in a left lead. These are things you can learn well only by doing them over and over yourself. As you learn them, so will your horse.

One thing I'd sure avoid: Don't run reining patterns on your colt all the time. He will start anticipating and ducking away. You just don't need to do a lot of Figure 8's on a young colt. Lots of the best reining horses never run the complete reining pattern (the American Quarter Horse Association pattern) until they come to a show. If he learns to rein, stop and change leads, he can run the pattern.

Spurs?

Most of the time I won't use spurs to break a colt. It just scares them. But most cowboys who work with horses all the time feel like they're half undressed if they don't wear them. Like a rooster they feel like they've just got to have them.

I have done this, though: Take a light pair of spurs and put tape around the rowels. That's not as severe. But most young horses won't even need that. The beginning rider *sure* doesn't need any spurs. That horse has enough trouble just putting up with that rider as he is. If the rider goes to spurring the horse and holding him with the reins at the same time, the horse wants to go someplace and there's no place to go but up. Instead of sharp spurs most young riders need sharp ideas.

7

Fat: Enemy of Performance

YOU'VE probably heard the old saying that "Fat is the prettiest color for a horse."

Well, maybe it is—if you want to lead that horse into a halter class or try to sell him for a good price. Most people will walk up and look at a horse and if he's real fat and slick, they'll say he's 'pretty.' If you took 150 pounds off .that horse you might have him down to where you could see what the *horse* looked like instead of the *fat*.

Ordinarily a horse will grow until he is seven years old. But I know some breeders who can make them almost fully grown by the time they're three. They feed them good and give them so much minerals, and everything else they need, that they'll look as 'finished' at three as they'll ever get.

A horse can be pushed too far and too fast, though, and it's not good for him. I never did like to see a horse get so fat that he was uncomfortable—and that is sure what will happen to him in hot weather if he's much overweight. It's as hard on him then as it is on a fat person. Besides that, if he carries too much weight, his feet can give out on him. When a young horse is carrying too much weight on his frame to start with, and you put your saddle and your own weight on him, he's apt to be overloaded.

I think it is possible that some two-year-old horses have been killed from overfeeding. I know for sure that some have bad legs from too much feed. In fact, you'd be surprised at the overfed and overfattened horses that will have splints on them before they're even broke to ride. This weight can also weaken him in the ankles or maybe not shape up in the body like he ought to.

This mare, although, she appears thin, is actually in good flesh to start performance training. She can be used without overheating.

Effect On Performance

The worst thing, though, is that it's hard to start a horse into much performance training if he is overweight. I believe in having a horse in good "living condition." I don't want him carrying 50 to 150 pounds of extra weight. If he is, then he doesn't feel any more like learning to do something than a man who's 25 pounds overweight.

Now I don't think it hurts to ride a fat horse pretty good in the winter, nearly anywhere. You can usually ride him long enough to teach him something. But in this part of the country—the Southwest —from June until about September is usually so hot you need to ride him early in the morning or at night. Otherwise, you can't ride *long enough* to teach him anything.

I don't mean to say that a fat horse isn't able to do *anything*. It's as natural for some horses to be fat as it is for some people. Some

This mare, although in fine shape for a halter show, should lose at least 50 pounds before starting any intensive performance work.

will stay fat all their lives. But not many. And some of the toughest horses I ever saw have never been overweight. This kind of horse can stand a whole lot. Usually he will have a lot of endurance and a lot of nerve.

Take a horse that's overweight and go to a cutting with him. He may be a trained cutting horse, but if the calves are tough and he really tries, he's apt to give out. Then if he slows up, and you let him slow up, he doesn't forget that. Next time, fat or lean, he may not try as hard.

What Is Overweight?

A lot of people, I know, won't have a good idea whether their horses are fat or not. The photographs on these pages may help give you an idea of what I think about when I call a horse fat and when I talk about one that's in performance condition.

Take the little buckskin mare that looks pretty thin. She is in about the right flesh to use without getting her too hot. She stands 14:1 and weighs 950 pounds as you see her in the photo. She would have to weigh over 1,000 pounds to show well in a halter class. And she is above average in conformation although she might have a little finer head. But over-all she's a clean-muscled pony, not muscle bound, and she'll make a good roping, reining or cutting horse.

Now look at the chestnut sorrel mare. She'll stand 14:1 also but she will weigh 1,025 or better and she's a little fat. She's a good-muscled mare but I don't like to ride this kind of pony hard in the summertime. I would want to take 50 pounds off of her before trying to teach her very much.

A horse's weight is going to depend on both size and the kind of bone structure he has. A horse that will weigh 1,000 pounds fully grown ought not to weigh more than about 700 as a yearling. That gives him 300 pounds to grow, over the next five or six years. But the way some horses are fed now, a 700 to 800 pound yearling may weigh more than 1,000 pounds as a three-year-old when he's not mature at all. I don't think this kind of feeding produces a long-lived horse.

Weight Control Means Exercise

In the case of the two mares you see pictured here, it isn't too hard to get the fat mare down to performance condition right away. You can pull 50 pounds off a 1,000 pound horse pretty easy. Haul her 500 miles by trailer and she may lose it all. But if you can trot her and get that fat *hard* then you're getting your horse in good shape.

As we discussed in another chapter, you can trot this overweight horse in a pen—I like a pen filled with deep sand—and if you'll do that every day you'll get your pony in good shape. Lots of times I'll trot a group of five or six horses in a pen together for 10 or 15 minutes. Then I'll saddle one of those horses to ride and he has the 'edge' off of him. Sometimes too, if he is a horse that I'm breaking, I'll ride him in the pen and follow the others around and make them trot. This young horse I'm riding gets the idea that he's *doing* something and that business of going in a circle doesn't get so monotonous to him.

Feed What They Clean Up

There's not much use to having your horse too fat in the first place. I think this happens sometimes because people admire their horses so much they want them to have the best—and they get extra generous with the feed bucket.

To give you an idea of what might be fed to a growing horse, we'll say your young mare weighs between 900 and 950 pounds. In the spring, summer and fall you can feed her a gallon of oats and a half a gallon of bran twice a day—along with all the dry hay she wants. I don't recommend alfalfa in the summer, though. That will heat her too much. I like prairie or bermuda grass hay.

In case you don't have a gallon bucket, you can figure that four 1-pound coffee cans of rolled oats will just fill up a gallon bucket. If you feed whole oats, which are less bulky, the gallon can will hold almost 5 coffee cans full.

On this ration, your mare will be getting roughly three gallons of feed a day. She may be able to eat 10 to 15 pounds of hay. If you are not riding her, she can get fat on this much. If you ride her enough, she won't get fat on it.

If she leaves some of her feed or hay, cut down a little bit on it. Feed her what she will clean up overnight. If there's a lot left in the trough next morning, cut back a little.

You can expect this to happen too: Your horse may be eating real good, then you start riding her every day. She will be apt to get off her feed a little bit. She won't eat as much that first week you ride her. Then in about 10 days she'll start eating more again—and wind up eating more than she did before you rode her.

I would not put any salt or minerals directly into the feed of any horse. They are like humans. What may suit one won't suit another. Horses should have salt where they can get to it and maybe a separate box of minerals. They will eat what they need.

Riding After Feeding

It may not be good for them but there are not very many people who will wait very long to ride their horses after they're fed. I have had to take some right away from the feed trough as they got through. We used to do our mules that way on the farm a long time ago; took them from the feed trough, hooked them up and went to work.

What can hurt a horse isn't just using him after he's eaten but getting him too hot. Changing his feed, then riding him hard, can also hurt him. This could make him sick even though you have been riding him every day. So I wouldn't change a horse's feed while you're training him. It wouldn't affect his learning but it sure might make him founder pretty easy.

When you do ride your horse hard he should be cooled before you water him. Keep him away from water at least until he has quit blowing and panting. If he just has a little sweat on him and he isn't blowing, water won't hurt him. You will notice when he is overheated that he will breath different—a lot harder.

Food As a Reward

When I used to work with trick horses I'd reward one I was teaching by giving him a piece of carrot or lump of sugar. But I never would give a horse something like that for any other reason. I'd rather have oats than anything. Just put a handful of oats in your pocket and it will do the same thing sugar will—only the sugar will finally

Fat: Enemy of Performance

spoil a horse to where everytime he sees you, he wants it.

But you can even overdo the oats reward. I sure wouldn't advise anybody to do that for a cutting, roping or performance horse. There's no need to reward a horse just because he's yours. You don't want one like a spoiled child—wanting something every time you turn around.

I'd rather reward a horse by petting him. If he does something right that you're teaching him, just pat him a couple of times on the neck and call his name. He can tell whether you're correcting him or petting him by the tone of your voice.

Now I wouldn't want anybody to think from all this that we keep the horses *hungry* at my house. A hungry horse is apt to be like a person—when I get hungry I get kind of aggravated. I know *I'd* be hard to train if I was sure enough hungry. But it's like putting gas in your tractor. You put in all the gas the tractor can *use* and no more. It doesn't take you long to find out how much your horse can eat— and *should* eat. Yet I know lots of my good friends who don't ever want their horses to see the bottom of that feed trough. This is because people are just as different as horses. An old boy may just be *determined* to get his horses fat and his girl friends skinny.

8

Starting The Roping Horse

A YOUNG horse that is "green-broke" can be started into roping when he's stout enough. This term green-broke means different things to different people. Some people will call a horse that after he's been ridden once or twice. They figure if they can get on and off the colt without being bucked off, then he's green-broke.

I'd call one green-broke if he has been ridden 60 days or so and handles pretty good, if you can work cattle on him, say, or just ride straight down the road. I have ridden colts 17 and 18 months old that you could do most anything on. They were taught from the start that they had to do some work nearly every day—something that was useful. One mare we have now weighs 1,320 and we were roping on her when she was 17 months old.

But you can't afford to forget that a colt of this age is still pretty much of a baby. You have to go slow at first. You take a young horse out and saddle him up, then lope off after a calf, swinging a rope, and the colt may buck with you.

Early Rope Training

You need to get a colt used to the *feel* of a rope on his body. Drag a loop across his body, over and around his hips. Get in the saddle and let the rope slide down along his body, behind him and under him. You need to be careful about this. The rope under him can cause a colt to get upset, which is not bad. You want that colt to respect the rope near his feet so he won't be so apt to get tangled up in it. They don't all react the same to it. Some will step over a rope and it won't excite them a bit. Others get their feet over a rope and try to run away.

Running a calf helps the roping horse become accustomed to swinging rope, "rating" and proper positioning behind calf.

Next, I'd sit on the colt and swing the rope and pitch it out on the ground so he can see it. Then rope something on the ground like a log or piece of brush but don't put any pressure on the horse from that. You might also ease up to a calf in a corner of the pen and toss the loop at the calf so that the rope hits him but doesn't catch him. Do this enough so the colt gets used to you throwing that loop from the saddle and doesn't get excited when it happens.

Next, you need to teach the colt to "rate" a calf—to follow one at the same speed and in position for you to later rope the calf. I'd rather run calves in a pen to start with. There are too many things in lots of pastures that can be dangerous for the young horse when he chases a calf: holes, wire and logs, for instance. The first few calves you actually rope may scare the colt. He doesn't know what this is all about and in a pasture he may get so excited that he'll try to run away.

Some horses can learn to follow and rate a calf in 20 to 30 minutes —to stay behind the calf, within roping distance, all the way down the pen. But others may take 30 days to learn it. Some of the best roping horses I've ridden were slow to learn this. You may find the colt will follow one, running straight just fine. And if the calf ducks off to the left, maybe he'll fall right in behind. But if the calf ducks to the right, the colt won't follow. They develop habits like that.

It is best to keep the colt running right behind the calf. As he gets older and you would rather rope a little to the right or left, depending on whether you are right or left handed, you can move him over either way just a little.

Some of these colts, when you first start, will follow a calf in a trot or slow lope, but the first calf that runs hard can scare the colt, especially if you throw your loop. It is best to just swing your loop until the colt has run a few fast ones, to know how it feels to really run.

Don't worry too much about whether you can see the calf around your colt's head, if you are directly behind the calf as you run him. If you start reining your horse one way or the other to see the calf, the colt will get the idea he is supposed to duck off one way or the other before you rope, later on. After you start roping, the colt may keep on ducking away. If you're a beginning roper you will learn to rope the calf most anyplace out there—and as the colt learns more it will be easier to put him in proper position. At this point you want to think more about running the calf straight and, later, stopping the colt straight.

Another thing: Some horses won't run good if they are girthed real tight. You want it snug of course but still I've seen horses with girths so tight they could hardly catch the calf. I like to use a breast harness too since some horses are built in such a way that a saddle will work back. Your horse can run with more ease and comfort if the saddle is well up on his withers with a breast harness to keep it there.

Breakaway Training

A breakaway device, in case you're not familiar with it, is fixed to let your lariat rope break away from the saddle horn when you rope something, then stop. It's a good way to get a colt used to a little pressure on him when he stops. You tie the end of your rope to a little piece of twine, then tie that to the saddle horn. Then put one calf in the pen and lope after him—and rope the calf.

Instead of stopping the horse suddenly, though, just slow him down enough so the twine breaks and the colt feels enough of a jerk to know the rope was tied. Even then, don't stop the horse but go ahead and follow the calf a little way. This way, you don't wear out your calves or drive your horse into the ground.

Go get your rope and do that a few more times on the colt, so he will get the idea that you mean to rope the calf and that he can expect a little jerk on the rope after you slow him down. If you rope and *miss* the calf, just keep tracking the calf and let the rope drag on the ground. The colt needs to get used to that rope dragging under and alongside him.

If it's not too hot, you can rope five or six calves breakaway the first day. I wouldn't rope any out of the chute, though. You're teaching him now just to *catch* a calf. That's all you want his mind on. Once he catches on to the breakaway idea, you can tie the rope to the horn with a little stronger twine. This increases the jolt the colt gets when you slow down after roping the calf. It also means he has to start coming more to a stop to break the twine. You will need to help him some to learn this.

Starting The Roping Horse

Stopping

As you start roping breakaway, you are not getting off your horse after you rope. You want the pony to learn what happens when the calf hits the end of that rope. He will start protecting himself as the heavier twine makes it harder to break. He will start getting his hindquarters down in back, his feet will go out in front. When he begins to do this, you can try leaving the saddle once after you rope. If he stops as he should he will naturally pull his shoulders back since he's looking for the calf to hit the end of the rope—and he is bracing himself.

This "suck back" is what breaks the twine as you make it heavier and harder to break. You are working him up to the point where he thinks he can break the rope every time you catch a calf. He feels the jolt, sees the calf run on and thinks that he has done something. How much these horses can use their shoulders to get back isn't always the same.

You may find a 900-pound horse that can really break a 36-strand rope—about the heaviest you will ever use for calves— where a horse weighing 1,250 stops just as hard but can't break it. The big horse doesn't have the "get-back" the little horse has.

Working the Rope

To put more of this ability in him, you might work the colt on a log or railroad cross-tie. You might nail blocks under it so you can rope the tie from horseback. Then ride up, rope the cross-tie (using an old rope) and toss out your slack. This slack, going by the colt's head, should tell him to stop and get back. Leave the saddle, then spook him a little so he'll get back against that rope. When you get near the cross-tie, pick up the rope at arm level and drop it. When he brings that cross-tie to you, step on it and add your weight. Teach him to stop then with the "Whoa" command.

The reason for all this is that you want him to jerk that calf when you have picked it up and help you get the animal off its feet. When it hits the ground you want him to stop with a tight rope, so you can tie the calf. The way this contest goes nowadays, every second counts and you can't dance around out there very long. So you don't want your rope horse to drag the calf, then step up and then get back again. If the rope goes slack the calf will raise his head and then kick as the rope tightens. The horse must learn that as you "leg" or "flank" the calf, and start up, that's his signal to hit the rope; as the calf hits the ground, he stops.

Another good way to make the colt work that rope is to go in a pen with a calf or light steer and rope one hind foot of the animal. Even a small calf, roped by one hind foot, will kick—and if there is any slack in the rope, your colt will sure get back. That slack hits the colt on the neck and he learns fast that the rope won't hit him if it is tight. Of course, *you* can also stand out there and hit him with

If the horse doesn't keep slack out of line the kicking calf will slap him on neck with loose rope. Notice colt's close attention.

the slack, but he soon gets to watching just you and not the calf. But with one hind leg of a calf hooked to that rope, he watches that calf pretty close and keeps back.

Next, you're ready to rope a few with the rope tied to the horn, so it *won't* break. On the young colt I like to start with staying in the saddle on the first few calves. I'll rope the calf, stop and then let somebody else turn the calf loose. This gives you time to keep the horse straight at the end of the rope.

As you get off the colt, later, to go down the rope and tie the calf, you will probably notice that he is working the rope even better than you expected. Usually he isn't just getting back because he wants to or knows he is supposed to but because of fright. He's trying to keep back from that calf. At first you may have to talk to him a few minutes and calm him down after you have roped on him. It is hard sometimes to ride him up to the calf to allow enough slack to turn the calf loose.

I should mention here that you don't need to just grind your pony into the ground when you are stopping him on these first few calves. When you rope your calf, the colt will be running on a loose rein most likely. Just take up a light but firm pressure on the rein and if he goes down behind, give him some slack on the reins. He's not supposed to stop until you pull up the slack in your lariat rope and pitch it up alongside his head. Your weight is still full in the saddle—and I think it is best to keep it there until the horse has felt the full jolt of the calf hitting the end of the rope. It might even be best to make him take two or three steps back, keeping him straight, before you go down to tie the calf.

The colt also needs to know how to work himself out of corners when working the rope. If you run a calf into a corner of the pen, then rope the calf as you come out, the horse winds up in the corner —usually backing up into the fence. He can't help you much there. So do that at home. Rope a calf coming out of a corner and spook the pony back into the fence a time or two. He will soon get to watching that fence and move off to one side or the other to avoid hitting it.

Starting The Roping Horse

Into the Chute

You see a lot of chute-crazy horses at ropings because lots of ropers don't take enough time with their first training. It's not a good idea to ride your colt in there and bust out after your first calf, full speed, with no preparation at all. I'd rather ride a colt into the roping chute, or box, when you don't intend to rope anything. Ride him in and stand him in there after you've been exercising him. Let him rest in the chute so he'll get used to it. While he's standing in there back him up so he gets used to the feel of the boards against his hocks and hindquarters. After a few days he won't think anything about going into the chute.

Then you can get some slow calves and turn one out and break your horse out at the same time. If it is a slow calf your colt will just walk or trot out of the chute. Don't hurry him. He won't know to really break out of there. But you won't turn out half a dozen calves before he will start naturally breaking out faster.

You wouldn't necessarily rope any of these first few calves, although if he was rating them good it shouldn't make any difference. But after you've run two or three calves a day for, say, a week, watch the colt— the first time he shows any sign of wanting to get excited in the chute, hold him in there, turn a calf loose and don't let him run it. This is what we call "scoring" a calf. You just sit there and hold him in the chute while the calf runs on down the arena. Then turn out another and keep turning them out, one by one, until he realizes that he doesn't have to run every calf. You don't want him all upset every time the gate rattles on the calf runway.

On these slow calves you would want to let them get a couple of jumps out there before you break your horse out of the box. Give them five or six feet start so the colt can see where the calf is going to go. Even if the calf doesn't run straight, with that short a "score" (or head start) the colt shouldn't have any trouble catching up and rating the calf. If you use fast calves and run him out of there at full speed every time, he'll soon get chute crazy, wanting to go.

After some scoring of calves you will start to see how your colt breaks best. Some can come out faster when they are standing straight in the chute. Others break better standing at a slight angle. The horse himself can show you which way he comes out best.

The Barrier

In the calf roping contest, they put a string barrier across the mouth of the chute. The calf with a line to the barrier, jerks it away when he reaches the proper score distance, and that is when you can come out after the calf. If the horse breaks the barrier before that then you are penalized 10 seconds.

So you need to get your colt used to the barrier being there and teach him it won't hurt him. You can do this by putting a barrier up and letting him walk through it without any calf being turned out.

This young horse shows good form in stopping: Hindquarters are going down as forefeet go out, his head is down and he is watching the calf. As rope tightens he will 'suck back' with his shoulders.

Put it up again and let him run through it. He will decide that little string doesn't hurt him. It just breaks. Some young horses won't pay any attention to it. Some older horses—that might have been tangled up in wire sometime—may fear it and may even try to jump over it.

You're not teaching him to break this barrier but just not to fear it. In the contest you want him to get as close to the barrier, as it opens, as you can, *without* breaking it. If he is afraid of it, he won't start near as fast. A slow horse that can leave that chute fast can catch a lot of calves quicker than a fast horse, over a short score.

Equipment

Besides what we've talked about, like a beast harness, I'd recommend you put heel boots on your roping horse. On hard ground he almost has to have them to protect ankles and heels—if he can *sure enough* stop. As for bits, most any kind is all right that a colt is used to and respects. But the roping horse is not like a real 'handling' horse such as the reining or cutting horse. He doesn't need to be as sensitive on the reins. So I'll train one for awhile with a regular hackamore bit—that's the hackamore with the shanks. Lots of roping horses don't wear anything but that. Some of this is in the horse's mouth and some is in his owner's head. Some ropers think a hackamore *looks* better on his horse. I'll use a hackamore bit on some horses but usually I wind up using a regular port bit on most. If a horse that can run gets wound up and really going you need a little more holding power in his mouth.

Mistakes

Many young ropers take a colt and try to rope too fast a calf and too many of them. That's what can discourage a horse to where he doesn't like roping at all. If you want to show your horse's speed, take him to a race track.

Another thing I see a lot is the roper who runs his horse out after a calf, misses the calf and spins his horse around right then. This can get a horse to where, whether you catch the calf or not, he will turn around after you throw your loop. That could be embarrassing. *You* might not stop.

9

Starting The Cutting Horse

THERE'S an important difference between the ranch cutting horse and the one you see at shows and rodeos. Your ranch horse goes into a herd of cattle and takes a cow out, then drives her—maybe 50 or 100 yards—to where men on horseback are holding 'the cut.' This means the cattle you are cutting out to sell, or ship or doctor.

Once the ranch horse has that cow pointed toward the cut he doesn't want her turning around or giving him any trouble.

In your arena cutting, the idea is for the cattle to *make* a contest out of it by turning around and trying to get past the horse, back into the herd. So the contest cutting horse takes the cow out of the herd and stops. Without any help from the rider, he is supposed to keep her from re-entering the herd. The turnback men on horseback drive the cow back to make her face the cutting horse. You want your contest horse to stand his ground if the cow charges him but not to go after her if she turns and runs toward the turnback men.

This cutting contest is one of the popular stock horse contests in America now. You'll find cutting contests held at the Quarter Horse shows all over the country, and there were more than 900 of these scheduled in 1963. Cutting is also held at many of the Appaloosa, Arabian and Paint Horse shows as well as the major rodeos. Once you have seen some of the good cuttings you will understand why you don't train a top cutting horse overnight. If you're not a trainer yourself you need to watch some of the professionals and see how they handle the contest on their horses. You can learn a lot watching the men who do this for a living.

He Must 'Handle' First

Before some horses are started on cattle, they have a tendency to be lazy. They won't respond quick. You need to have them where they respond to the slightest touch of your legs or reins, so they will move in an instant. This isn't easy and you may have to try different bits and learn all you can about your horse's temperament to get him to handling. Sometimes it can take 20 or 30 days of daily work.

You will find some good cutting horses that are not reining horses and don't handle well. Yet they have so much "cow sense" they make up for that. You won't know what kind of horse you have at first. But if he is bred for cow work—that is, if his sire or dam were cutting horses—then there's a good chance this colt will have cow sense.

This is something a horse almost has to have to do well in cutting. He must be *interested* in cattle and *want* to work them. You can tell sometimes how much cow sense a horse has by taking him to cattle and watching his reactions. If he starts to study those cattle and pays a lot of attention, it is a good sign.

He Has to Run

In training a young horse for cutting, the first thing I want to know is whether the colt can run. If he can't run at first, he needs to learn. He should be able to break and run from a standing start and be able to gather his speed in 30 yards or less. That's about as far as most cutting horses will have to run to "head" (or turn) a cow. I think the horse needs to know how to run before you ever start him on cattle. Then he will know he *can* run.

There are cutting horses that never learned to run. You will see this kind of horse head a cow all right but then he'll just jump around in front of the cow. If she can move and makes a break for the fence, he's lost.

So I'd teach a colt to run and stop and turn back at a pretty good speed. Here, I'm talking about a horse that is well-broke and handles as he should. One good test for him is to run the horse toward a fence, stop, roll back and come away running. If a cow beats you to the fence she will have the length of the horse's neck to go between him and the fence. If he can really drive to the fence and at an angle, he can stop up the gap—then he has to be able to roll back and come away fast. So find out first how he can move, gather himself and stop on both fences. Also run him into a corner and come out running. When he can do that smooth and fast, he's ready to see some cattle.

Work at a Distance

I would rather start a young horse on cattle without any turnback horses. If you start right into arena conditions your colt may be interested—but when the turnback horses start to *make* the cattle move toward him, first thing you know your horse will be watching

Starting a young mare into cutting, Sikes uses no turnback men and rides mare with hackamore. No great 'action' is demanded here— mare is being taught only to keep calf away from herd.

the turnback horses more than the cattle. This will cause him to move before the cow does.

So it is better to get a few fresh cattle off by yourself. It can be in a pen or off in one corner of a pasture. Pick out a slow cow and head her off from the herd. All you want to teach the colt at this point is to keep that cow away from the herd. You don't need to have him up close to the cow to do it. Doesn't matter if she is 50 feet or more from your horse. You can't expect him to really get his head down and start working her this soon. That will come later. For now you're showing him only one thing: Keep her out of that herd. With no turnback men the cow will keep her distance out there. All you need to do is be patient and move your colt only when the cow moves, just enough to block her away from the herd.

51

Starting The Cutting Horse

I have started colts by driving cattle across open country and it's a pretty good way to start one. Whenever you drive cattle any distance at all you will find that at least one old cow will always drag along. She won't keep up with the rest. You can pick out that cow for your colt to drive. She will stop occasionally and you can move the colt over there and make her go on. It won't be very long before, when she stops, he will move over by himself and move her. He gets the idea that she is supposed to go with the rest of the cattle, and he begins to understand how to handle them.

After some pasture work you might try this: Take a small herd into a pen then cut the cattle out one at a time and drive them

Caught out of position, mare is reined sharply to right to block calf from herd. On young horses, most trainers will cut the slower cattle that colts can handle with ease.

through a gate to another pen, as a ranch horse would do it. This gives your young horse more to do and he soon understands that each cow is not supposed to come back to the herd once he has taken her away from it.

When he knows that, you might try him on a cow that will turn around. Drive one out of the herd 50 or 60 feet and stop the colt. If the cow doesn't turn back and face your horse, let that cow return to the herd—then you go back in and bring out another cow. When a cow will face your horse, he will try harder to work her. So if she gives him some "play"—that is, if she tries to get by him—don't quit her unless she turns away.

In the Arena

Once you decide to start work in a pen, you don't have to use a whole herd of cattle on a young horse that is just learning. I usually just put one cow in there. That not only helps the horse but the cattle as well. You can tire out your cattle even though you may not work them all.

If you have two pens side by side, you can have your herd of cattle in one and take your horse and one cow in the other. She will usually try to get to the fence through which she can see the other cows. You don't want to put on a big show here—just keep that cow out in the pen, as far from the other cattle as you can.

I don't mean you *have* to use cattle. Lots of the boys use goats and I have used them too. You can use sheep too, although goats are better. In fact, a horse may watch a goat where he may not watch a cow. He will also sure enough watch a hog. I have worked cutting horses on hogs and some will work a hog and get their heads lower than on any animal. They will even work geese, turkeys and chickens. I had one mare once that would work a feed sack.

We got 100 feet of rope and tied the feed sack in the middle of it, and put a man at each end with the rope across the arena. They would drag that sack back and forth across in front of that mare and she would head that sack just as she would a cow. And she was just starting into cutting.

So you can actually start horses on anything that will move although you can't beat the live animal—the cow, steer, calf or goat.

Additional Tips

If the weather is hot, you need to be careful not to overwork a young horse on cattle. In the contest, you will have two-and-a-half minutes to work your cattle. That gives you time to cut out about three head and work them right. Even a trained cutting horse can get to breathing hard if the cattle are active, after that kind of workout. So if it's hot, you shouldn't work over two or three head, once you start really working your colt.

It is important at this stage too that you show him the things he *can't* do—like biting the cattle or letting them go too far by him or watching something outside the arena.

At first, this green colt tries to watch too many things: the cow, the 'obstacle' bucket and even horses penned in the background. But these distractions can speed up the horse's education.

You might want to put some 'obstacles' in the pen so the colt will have some distractions to put up with. You can put out some rubber buckets in the arena or maybe hang a black coat on the fence. Even a few feed sacks thrown on the fence will make things look different to him. You want him able to concentrate on those cattle. At cuttings you will go to later on there will be lots of new sights and sounds; if he's not used to changes, they can bother him in the contest.

Always try to "quit" your cattle when your horse is in a good position. As you have seen at cuttings, most of the riders signal the horse to quit by touching his neck, then going back into the herd for another cow.

Some contestants, though, don't make their horses go ahead and work out of tight spots. They feel a cow is getting ahead of them and their horse is about to get "in a storm." So they quit the cow and pull up in a bad position. They pull up thinking maybe the judge won't know the difference. But they don't help a horse by doing that. If a horse quits every time he gets in a tight spot, or because a cow is too rank, he'll learn to quit, period. He'll figure out that when things get hard he can just ease off and let the cow get

Later, accustomed to the sights and sounds around him, the colt settles down and gives his full attention to the job at hand. In contests, he will need to be able to work under all conditions.

away. So, especially at home, you want to go ahead and make him hold that cow out there. Even in a contest I'd rather see you let your horse *lose* a cow completely while really *trying* to hold one than quit a cow in a bad position.

The way you approach a herd can be mighty important too. Let's say you get a cow out there that really runs and your horse heads her from one side to the other as fast as he can move; if that cow turns and runs to the other end of the arena, don't just wheel your colt around and plow back into that herd. Keep him facing the way that cow went for a little bit. Then turn him around and let him face the herd—and also let him catch his breath. Then just ease back into the herd while you pick out the next cow you want.

To score well, you're going to have to go deep into the herd for at least one head. Most judges are watching to see how well you can get in and out of the herd with the least disturbance to that herd. That is part of the whole idea of the contest.

A lot of us don't ride *through* the herd near as much as we should. We sometimes pick the first cow we get to, since we're worried about running out of time. Just remember: Lots of cuttings have been won by horses that only worked two head of cattle; very few have been won by horses that worked four head.

Starting The Cutting Horse

The Rules

Here are the official judging rules for cutting, as set forth by The National Cutting Horse Association:

1. A horse will be given credit for his ability to enter a herd of cattle and bring one out with very little disturbance to the herd or to the one brought out. If he (or his rider) creates unnecessary disturbance throughout his working period, he will be penalized.
2. When an animal is cut from the herd, it must be taken toward the center of the arena. If it goes down the arena fence, that is all right, but the horse should never get ahead of the animal and duck it back toward the herd to get more play but should let the turnback man turn it back to him.
3. A horse will be penalized 2 points each time the back arena wall is used for turnback purposes; the back fence to be agreed on and designated by the judge or judges before the contest starts; meaning the actual fence only, no imaginary line from point to point to be considered. If any of the contestants voice an objection, before the contest starts, the judge or judges shall take a vote of the contestants, and a "back fence" acceptable to the majority shall be designated and used.
4. If a horse runs into, scatters the herd, lanes or circles the herd against the arena fence, while trying to head an animal, he will be penalized heavily.
5. If a horse turns the wrong way with tail toward animals, he will be disqualified for that go-round with no score.
6. A horse will be penalized 1 point each time he is reined or cued in any manner. If he is reined or cued several times during a performance, he will be penalized each time. When a horse is picked up hard with the reins and set over, or reined, cued excessively, or spurred in the shoulder, a heavier penalty will be marked against him.
7. For riding with a tight rein through a performance, a penalty will be given; for part of the time during a performance, less penalty.
8. If a horse lets an animal that he is working get back in the herd, he will be penalized 5 points.
9. When a horse heads an animal and goes past it to the degree that he loses his working advantage, he will be penalized each time he does so. If a horse goes past as much as his length, he will be assessed a heavier penalty. Unnecessary roughness, such as a horse losing his working position to paw or bite cattle, will be penalized.
10. If a contestant quits an animal he is working when the horse is out of position, or the animal has an undue advantage of the horse, he will be penalized 3 points.
11. A judge marks from 60 to 80 points. An average performance should be marked around 70. A judge should be careful not to mark an average performance too high because the next horse that shows may put on a top performance that deserves 5 or 6 points above average, and if the average performance was marked 75, that would leave no room to give the top horse the credit he deserved above the other.

•

Winning points will be based on a horse's ability to work cattle and the amount of play he gets from the animal during the performance. In other words, if a horse gets good play and shows plenty of ability to cut cattle and the judge thinks he deserves a 78 marking for what he did but he assessed a three-point penalty against him for reining, he would mark him 75.

10

Sportsmanship

ONE TROPHY that every horse show ought to give, I think, is a trophy for sportsmanship. It should be given to the exhibitor who shows in more than one class and, by the way he handles his horse *and himself,* makes it plain that he knows what good sportsmanship means. I'm not sure an adult should be entitled to such an award. Adults are old enough to *know* how to act. But this kind of award teaches children. And I know from experience that a kid who wins a sportsmanship trophy is prouder of that than anything he will ever win at a horse show.

I'm glad to see lots of shows already giving such an award. Usually they will have one or two judges, who are unknown to everyone else, watching each halter and performance class. After the show is over they usually announce which exhibitor has won the sportsmanship award. It is awarded to the *person,* not his horse. But if a youngster has a good horse and if he wins that sportsmanship trophy, he is capable of winning nearly anything.

More Sportsmanship Needed

Since I judge a lot of shows I see a lot of sportsmanship, good and bad. Most of what I see is good. But you do see people griping because they don't win—and it's sometimes because they don't understand about how horses are judged.

That horse of yours won't work the same way every time you take him into a performance class and he won't *look* the same to every judge who sees him in a halter class. I may like a horse well enough to put him first in his class but another judge, next week, may think he belongs in third or fourth. He may like a little bit different type of horse. And that's fine. If we all liked the same kind of horse, exactly, we couldn't have many horse shows. If we all liked only one kind of automobile there wouldn't be but one kind pretty soon. The others would go broke.

And yet you will find adults who will win with a horse in a halter class a couple of times and they will then expect they should win at every show. You have a lot of people who start liking a horse more all the time just because they own him. They would be like a man who loves his wife. Another fellow might not care a thing for her.

Many people know exactly what faults their horses have—yet they either hope they are wrong or else they hope nobody will see those faults.

For instance, a woman once showed her horse where I was judging and the horse didn't place. Later she asked me what I didn't like about the horse.

"What is it about your horse that *you* don't like?" I asked her.

"Well," she said, "I don't like his neck. It's too big."

I said, "You're right. He's too big in front and not big enough behind." She already knew her horse's weakness.

The Judge's Job

Finding flaws in how a horse is built or how he performs is what they pay a judge to do. They don't invite a judge to a show so he can find just the *good* things about the horses there. He is supposed to see the things that are wrong too. Most judges, if they are qualified, can do this pretty quick.

A judge can stand in the middle of the show ring and let them lead 20 horses in there. By the time the last horse has entered the arena he will know which horse he wants to put in first place—that is, if he is a horseman and if he is honest. He will spot his winner almost immediately.

So you ask, "Why then do you spend so much time judging the class?"

For two reasons: One is that it will take a while to place the other horses in the order you think they should be. If I'm judging a show I just pretend to myself that, in every class, they are going to *give* me six horses (or however many placings they have) and I can take them home with me. Well, if they *were* going to give me the best six horses in each class, don't you know I'll try to pick the six very best horses out of that class?

I'm not going to pick ole' Ben's horse just because Ben owns him. I will pick the horses *I* like. And I don't think a judge should pay any attention to who is leading the horse, whether it is man or woman, boy or girl. He is supposed to judge only the horses.

This is where sportsmanship is a two-way street. Not only should the exhibitor show respect for the judge's opinion but *he* should respect *them* too. And that's the second reason most judges will take time to inspect every horse there, even though he may already know which one he likes the best.

For all the judge knows, this may be the first time you have ever shown a horse in a show. You paid your entry fee like everybody else. If he walks by your horse without really looking at your horse, you wouldn't feel very good about it. But if your horse does get inspected—as much as the horse that later wins—then you feel as if you have not been overlooked. Then if your horse doesn't win at three or four shows you won't be too discouraged. You will start to understand what kind of horse the judges like and will want to get one that has a better chance to win or place.

Maybe this is not so much sportsmanship on the judge's part as a matter of common courtesy.

Seek Good Criticism

Speaking for myself, I sure don't mind it when exhibitors come to me after the show and ask me to criticize their horses—to tell them what I like or don't like about them. Sometimes this is not easy. I've had people bring horses to me and ask my opinion—and that pony of theirs may be very little horse. If he is a pretty decent kind of horse I'll say so. If he just isn't, though, I may be tempted to talk about fishing or hunting—and I don't do either one.

But seriously, most judges are glad to tell you what they think are good and bad points about your horse—and most will tell you his is just *one* opinion. Others will have different opinions. And keep in mind always that halter show judging, in particular, is exactly that: One man's opinion.

When I think about it, I guess I've never seen a horse yet that I couldn't find *something* good about. It might just be his eyes. Or I might like his color. Hardly ever do I see a horse that doesn't have some little something that I like.

I guess maybe I'm sympathetic to all horses because I have owned some that were so ugly their mamas could hardly love them. Yet they could usually *do* something. They didn't win many beauty contests but they were good horses nevertheless.

Other publications of the

CORDOVAN CORPORATION

The Texas and Southwestern Horseman

The southwest's monthly Magazine of Western Riding is a lively informative guide to buying, training, enjoying and winning with a western horse. Each month there is news of Quarter Horse, Appaloosa, Pinto and other breed competitions, as well as news of open shows, cuttings, ropings, barrel races and rodeo. Features important "how to" articles by and with the nation's leading stock horse trainers plus tips on horse production and care from outstanding breeders. Subscription: 1 year $3, 2 years $5, 3 years $7.

Championship Barrel Racing

The first comprehensive book on the country's exciting new stock saddle sport, written by World Champion Barrel Racer Jane Mayo and Texas Horseman Editor Bob Gray. With action photos, this book tells you essentials of recognizing a good barrel horse, starting a young one, barrel footwork, speed and its control—plus many hauling and contest tips that will help you win more often in competition. $4.00

Western Riding Games and Contests

Here is the long awaited book that tells you the rules and techniques for staging and competing in America's most popular stock saddle contests. In plain language with dramatic action photos, the book gives not only contest regulations, but important suggestions on horse training and handling for various competitions. Chapters cover cutting, roping, stake race, pole bending, barrel racing, baton relay, flag race, keyhole race, potato race, ring race, reining, rescue race, wagon race and prairie stump race. By Bob Gray $3.00

CORDOVAN CORPORATION

Cypress, Texas   Telephone Houston OV 6-8471